W9-BUK-831

Muhlenberg County Libraries
117 S. Main
Greenville, Kentucky 42345

DATE DUE

HIP-HOP

Tupac

Hal Marcovitz

Mason Crest Publishers

Tupac

FRONTIS The rapper, poet, and actor Tupac Shakur (1971–1996) has become a
hip-hop icon. Since his tragic death, a new generation of fans has learned
to enjoy Tupac's music.

PRODUCED BY 21ST CENTURY PUBLISHING AND COMMUNICATIONS, INC.

MASON CREST PUBLISHERS INC.
370 Reed Road
Broomall, Pennsylvania 19008
(866)MCP-BOOK (toll free)
www.masoncrest.com

Printed in Malaysia.

First Printing

9 8 7 6 5 4 3 2 1

Library of Congress Cataloging-in-Publication Data

Marcovitz, Hal.
  Tupac / Hal Marcovitz.
    p. cm. — (Hip-hop)
  Includes bibliographical references and index.
ISBN-13: 978-1-4222-0130-5
ISBN-10: 1-4222-0130-9
  1. Shakur, Tupac, 1971–1996—Juvenile literature. 2. Rap musicians—
United States—Biography—Juvenile literature. I. Title.II. Series.
ML3930.S48.M37 2007
782.421649092—dc22
[B]   2006011448

Contents

Hip-Hop Timeline

1974 Hip-hop pioneer Afrika Bambaataa organizes the Universal Zulu Nation.

1988 *Yo! MTV Raps* premieres on MTV.

1970s Hip-hop as a cultural movement begins in the Bronx, New York City.

1985 *Krush Groove*, a hip-hop film about Def Jam Recordings, is released featuring Run-D.M.C., Kurtis Blow, LL Cool J, and the Beastie Boys.

1970s DJ Kool Herc pioneers the use of breaks, isolations, and repeats using two turntables.

1979 The Sugarhill Gang's song "Rapper's Delight" is the first hip-hop single to go gold.

1986 Run-D.M.C. are the first rappers to appear on the cover of *Rolling Stone* magazine.

1970   **1980**   **1988**

1976 Grandmaster Flash & the Furious Five pioneer hip-hop MCing and freestyle battles.

1986 Beastie Boys' album *Licensed to Ill* is released and becomes the best-selling rap album of the 1980s.

1970s Break dancing emerges at parties and in public places in New York City.

1982 Afrika Bambaataa embarks on the first European hip-hop tour.

1988 Hip-hop music annual record sales reaches $100 million.

1970s Graffiti artist Vic pioneers tagging on subway trains in New York City.

1984 *Graffiti Rock*, the first hip-hop television program, premieres.

1993 Rapper Snoop Dogg's album *Doggystyle* is the first debut album to hit the music charts at number one.

2006 Queen Latifah becomes the first hip-hop artist to receive a star on the Hollywood Walk of Fame.

1989 DJ Jazzy Jeff & The Fresh Prince become the first hip-hop artists to win a Grammy Award.

2003 Rapper Eminem becomes the first hip-hop artist to win an Academy Award.

2005 Hip-hop artist Kanye West appears on the cover of *Time* magazine.

1989 Rap is added as a new category to the *Billboard* charts.

1997 East Coast rapper Notorious B.I.G. (aka Biggie Smalls) is murdered.

2004 First National Hip-Hop Political Convention is held in Newark, New Jersey.

1989   2000   2006

1990s Hip-hop emerges in Europe.

1996 West Coast rapper Tupac Shakur is shot and killed.

2005 Rapper Will Smith opens the Philadelphia Live 8 concert as part of 10 simultaneous concerts held worldwide to bring attention to the extreme poverty in Africa.

1989 First gangsta rap album, *Straight Outta Compton*, is released by N.W.A.

2001 The hip-hop political action group, Hip-Hop Summit Action Network, is founded by Russell Simmons.

2006 The Smithsonian Institute National Museum of American History announces the creation of a new hip-hop exhibition scheduled to open in three to five years.

1992 Dr. Dre's album *The Chronic* is released; it redefines West Coast rap.

By November 1994, Tupac had become one of hip-hop's biggest stars. His first three albums had been critically and commercially successful. In addition, he had appeared in several movies, drawing praise for his acting ability.

◀ 1 ▶

Against the World

After just three years as a rap artist, there was no brighter star in hip-hop than Tupac Shakur. He had good looks, talent as a showman, and a commanding presence on stage. Tupac's gritty **lyrics** about the hard life on inner city streets struck a chord with young hip-hop fans.

His talents were much in demand by other rappers, who often asked him to provide backup vocals for their albums. One up-and-coming rapper whom Tupac agreed to help was Little Shawn, a young and talented New York City **MC**. Late on the night of November 30, 1994, Tupac arrived at a recording studio on Times Square in New York City, where Little Shawn's album was in production.

Tupac's contribution to Little Shawn's album was sure to give the record a boost. Tupac's first three albums of gangsta rhymes had established the 23-year-old as a star. He had created a unique identity as a rebel, telling stories about troubled youth, street violence, and taking revenge against those who had wronged him. Tupac's life mirrored his music: he had been arrested

9

several times for committing violent acts and was in the middle of a court case when he agreed to record for Little Shawn. Tupac had been accused of sexual assault by a female fan and was out on bail awaiting the verdict.

Tupac arrived at the Times Square recording studio just past midnight. He was accompanied by his sister, Sekyiwa; her boyfriend, Zayd Turner; his manager, Freddie Moore; and another rapper, Stretch Walker. Tupac later said that things didn't look right as they entered the building—a suspicious-looking man was loitering outside. The man followed the group as they went inside. In the lobby, Tupac saw two more shady characters. As Tupac and his crew approached the elevator, the three strangers pulled out guns.

The men went straight for Tupac. They ordered him to the floor and demanded that he give up his money and jewelry. Instead, Tupac reached for a gun that he carried in his waistband. When the assailants saw him reach for his weapon, they opened fire. The rap star was hit five times: twice in the groin, twice in the head, and once in the left hand. Miraculously, none of the wounds proved fatal. But the assailants were not finished. They beat and kicked Tupac several times before robbing him, taking some $35,000 in jewelry. Later, in an interview with *Vibe* magazine, Tupac described the incident:

> **"I dropped to the floor. Everything in my mind said, 'Pac, pretend you're dead.' It didn't matter. They started kicking me, hitting me. I never said, 'Don't shoot!' I was quiet . . . I had my eyes closed, but I was shaking, because the situation had me shaking. And then I felt something in the back of my head, something real strong. I thought they stomped me or pistol-whipped me, and they were stomping my head against the concrete. I saw white, just white. I didn't hear nothing, I didn't feel nothing, and I said, 'I'm unconscious.' But I was conscious.**
>
> **And then I felt it again, and I could hear things now and I could see things and they were bringing me back to consciousness. Then they did it again, and I couldn't hear nothin'. And I couldn't see nothing; it was just all white. And then they hit me again, and I could hear things and I could see things and I knew I was conscious again."**

When armed robbers confronted Tupac in the lobby of Quad Recording Studio in Manhattan, the rapper reached for a concealed gun. Before he could draw the weapon, Tupac was shot five times.

Tupac's manager, Freddie Moore was hit by a gunshot and robbed as well. The assailants did not attack Tupac's sister and her boyfriend or Stretch Walker. It was clear that Tupac was the intended target.

Gangsta Rivalry

Despite his wounds, Tupac managed to rise to his feet. A police car was pulling up to the studio as the elevator door in the lobby opened. Tupac, Turner, and Walker stumbled into the elevator while Sekyiwa and Moore waited for police in the lobby. Tupac and the others rode to the eighth-floor recording studio where Little Shawn and his producers were waiting. Still conscious, Tupac started making wild accusations that he had been set up—that somebody knew he was coming and had arranged the shooting and robbery. Other people wearing jewelry as expensive as his had been in and around the building, but none of them got robbed, he ranted. Someone called an ambulance, and Tupac was rushed to the hospital. There, he underwent surgery on his wounds.

It was true that many people in the building knew Tupac had been scheduled to participate in Little Shawn's recording. The Times Square address served as the home of Quad Studios, which produced albums and videos on five floors of the building. Word had spread throughout the studios that Tupac would be arriving. "Everybody was all excited about 'Pac comin' in," record company executive Andre Harrell told a reporter from *Vibe*.

While Tupac was being shot in the lobby, the rap producer Sean "Puffy" Combs and his biggest star, Notorious B.I.G., were at work on a music video in an upstairs studio. Tupac and Notorious B.I.G. had always been friendly, despite being on opposite sides of a growing rivalry between Combs and a west coast rap producer named Marion "Suge" Knight, who was coming to have a great influence on Tupac.

The investigation into the incident revealed that a security camera inside the lobby was pointed at the door. This was so those inside could see who was arriving and buzz them into the building. This meant that the assailants had been buzzed in as well and strongly suggested that the attack was indeed a setup. However, the police never confiscated the tapes and surveillance camera, and the investigation was quickly dropped.

After recovering from his wounds, Tupac accused Biggie of setting up the shooting and robbery. Biggie denied the accusation. Still, the

Rapper Biggie Smalls—also known as Notorious B.I.G.— poses at the 1995 Billboard Music Awards ceremony in Las Vegas. Tupac and Biggie had once been friends. However, Tupac came to believe that Biggie had been involved in the shooting at Quad Recording Studio.

Tupac arrives at a New York courthouse on December 1, 1994, the day after being shot. He had checked himself out of the hospital to attend the hearing. The wheelchair-bound rapper was found guilty of sexual assault and sentenced to prison.

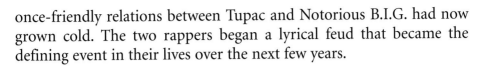

once-friendly relations between Tupac and Notorious B.I.G. had now grown cold. The two rappers began a lyrical feud that became the defining event in their lives over the next few years.

Against the World

Tupac checked himself out of the hospital the day after his surgery so that he could attend court and hear the jury's verdict in his sexual assault case. He heard the sentence while sitting in a wheelchair. Tupac was convicted. A few months later, he received a lengthy jail term at the Clinton Correctional Facility in upstate Dannemora, New York.

While in prison, Tupac's fourth album, *Me Against the World*, was released. It immediately hit the top of the hip-hop charts. The songs were filled with **introspection**, as Tupac found himself looking forward to a future filled with darkness and uncertainty. Some of the songs, including "So Many Tears," "Death Around the Corner," and "If I Die 2Nite," were visions of how Tupac expected his life to end. But it was the title track that made it clear to the hip-hop world that he intended to live his way, even if it led to his own death. The song included the lyrics:

> **"Can you picture my prophecy?**
> **Stress in the city, the cops is hot for me**
> **The projects is full of bullets, the bodies is droppin'**
> **There ain't no stoppin me. . . .**
>
> **The question is will I live? No one in the world loves me**
> **I'm headed for danger, don't trust strangers**
> **Put one in the chamber whenever I'm feelin' this anger**
> **Don't wanna make excuses, cause this is how it is"**

The future he saw for himself was not one of luxury, riches, and fame. He predicted violence, bloodshed, and death on the streets that had raised him.

Afeni Shakur (standing next to her son Tupac) was a member of the Black Panther Party, an organization formed to fight racism and help African Americans gain equality. The group was controversial because it used violence and intimidation to achieve its goals.

2

Born Rebel

When Tupac Shakur was 10 years old and living in a tough New York City neighborhood, a minister asked him what he wanted to be when he grew up. The boy did not hesitate to answer. He said, "A revolutionary." Even as a young child, his dissatisfaction and rebellious nature were evident.

His mother was born Alice Faye Williams but changed her name to Afeni Shakur when she joined the Black Panther Party in the 1960s. The civil rights movement had become a powerful force in the United States during the 1960s, but while black leaders like the Rev. Martin Luther King Jr. encouraged the use of nonviolent methods in the fight for equal rights, some groups had more radical notions about how to achieve equality for blacks. The Black Panthers were one such group. Members believed that blacks should resort to armed confrontation to achieve equality with whites. The Panthers gained notoriety because of their stance and influence. The organization was eventually dissolved after a series of police and FBI crackdowns.

Afeni Shakur was caught up in one such crackdown. In 1969 she was arrested and jailed along with 20 other Panthers on armed robbery charges. While awaiting trial in a New York City jail in late 1970, Afeni discovered she was pregnant. The father was Billy Garland, another member of the Panthers. Afeni and Billy never married, and he played no role in raising the child.

The police had a weak case against Afeni. She represented herself in court, and when the **prosecution's** chief witness took the stand, she was able to prove that he had never seen her commit a crime. Afeni and 13 others were found not guilty.

A month after Afeni's release from jail, on June 16, 1971, her son was born. She gave him the name Lesane Parish Crooks but soon changed his name to Tupac Amaru Shakur. The name was taken from Túpac Amaru II, a revolutionary in Peru during the 1780s. The native Inca people of Peru had been conquered by Spanish conquistadors during the 16th century. Túpac Amaru II was a descendant of the last Incan leader in Peru, and the revolutionary fought against Spanish colonists on behalf of the oppressed natives. His revolt was quickly crushed, and the Incan royal line was exterminated. It was probably Túpac Amaru's belief in equality and his desire to change the social order that prompted Afeni Shakur to adopt the name for her son.

As a former member of the Black Panthers, Afeni Shakur found few opportunities open to her in New York. She had trouble finding a job, so the first few years of her son's life were spent in a variety of rooms and apartments. To add to the stress, Tupac's half-sister Sekyiwa was born in 1975. The family was constantly on the move, occasionally homeless, and often forced to accept government assistance when they found themselves in desperate need of food and shelter.

Developing His Talent

Despite the lack of stability, Tupac managed to find opportunities to develop his talent as a performer. Afeni enrolled her 12-year-old son in a local theater group. Within a year Tupac earned a major role in the play *A Raisin in the Sun,* a drama about the struggles of a black family. Tupac played Travis, the son of the play's protagonists. *A Raisin in the Sun* explores how money affects people's emotional lives. Travis's father can only equate happiness to money, and he passes along that dysfunction to his young son. The play was performed at the world-famous Apollo Theater in Harlem.

In 1985 Afeni moved the family to Baltimore, Maryland, where she had been promised a job. Tupac enrolled in Rolling Park Junior High School, which he attended through the eighth grade. He was then accepted to the Baltimore School for the Arts (BSA), where he would have the opportunity to attend classes in acting, dance, and voice. Tupac's admission to BSA enabled him to truly start learning how to be

Tupac poses with a toy gun in a photo taken during the late 1970s. His half-sister Sekyiwa is on the right, wearing the pink coat. The Shakur family had little money, and moved often as Afeni tried to earn a living.

a performer. He wrote poetry, studied ballet, and acted in several plays. It was also during this period that Tupac started writing rap lyrics. While at the Baltimore School for the Arts, he often tried out his rhymes on the stage during school productions.

While attending BSA, Tupac formed a friendship with Jada Pinkett, a young and attractive drama student who would go on to become a movie star in her own right. Jada and Tupac both came from troubled homes and shared a desire to use their talents to break away from **ghetto** life. "We were a lot alike in a lot of ways. . . . Very opinionated, very passionate," Jada later recalled. "And basically just wanting 'our way or no way.'" She told *Holler If You Hear Me* author Michael Eric Dyson:

> **"He was poor. I mean, when I met Tupac, and this is not an exaggeration, he owned two pairs of pants, and two sweaters. Okay? He slept on a mattress with no sheets when I went to his room, and it took me a long time to get into his house because he was embarrassed. He didn't know where his meals were coming from."**

Life in the Jungle

While living in Baltimore, Afeni started using crack cocaine, prompting constant fights between mother and son. Her drug use affected Tupac's life greatly and had a lasting impact on his personality and interpersonal relationships. According to Jada Pinkett:

> **"[He was] really rough on Afeni. And you know, he took every opportunity to punish anybody who he felt didn't do right by him, by his standards. That came from his relationship with Afeni. . . . Your mother is your pulse to the world. And if that pulse ain't right, ain't much else going to be right."**

During the summer of 1988, a boy in Tupac's neighborhood was shot and killed. Fearing for the safety of her children, Afeni put Tupac and Sekyiwa on a bus and sent them across country to Marin City, California, to stay with a family friend. Marin City turned out to be a ghetto located in the otherwise affluent Marin County near San Francisco. Afeni joined them later and found a home for the family in

While attending the Baltimore School for the Arts, Tupac
became friends with another talented young performer, Jada
Pinkett. At the school, Jada studied dance and choreography.
She later pursued an acting career, appearing in such films as
Menace II Society and *Set It Off*.

When Tupac was about 17, he and his sister moved from Baltimore to California. The Shakurs settled in a tough neighborhood of Marin City nicknamed the Jungle. Many of Tupac's lyrics draw on his experiences in the ghetto of Marin City.

a drug- and gang-infested Marin City neighborhood that the police called the "Jungle."

Tupac lived with Afeni for just a short time. Her drug habit had grown worse. And Tupac never felt accepted in the Jungle. Because he dressed shabbily and wouldn't play basketball, he was often roughed up by neighborhood gang members.

Tupac attended the local school, Tamalpais High School, where he impressed teachers with his talent as an actor. Soon, though, he lost interest in his studies and dropped out of school at age 17. He took a job delivering pizzas and moved out of Afeni's home, finding a place to live with some friends in a vacant apartment. Tupac and his roommates formed a rap group—the One Nation Emcees.

It was while living in these **destitute** conditions that Tupac Shakur found his voice as a rapper. He drew his inspiration from the streets— the drug deals, robberies, murders, and other urban woes that surround many poor black youths. He was part of a growing movement in hip-hop known as "gangsta rap." Exemplifying this movement was a song written by Tupac and his friends entitled "Thug Life." In an interview on KMEL radio in San Francisco, Tupac said:

> **"[They were] just giving truth to the music. Being in Marin City was like a small town, so it taught me to be more straightforward with my style. Instead of being so metaphorical with the rhyme, I was encouraged to go straight at it and hit it dead on and not waste time trying to cover things. In Marin City, everything was straightforward. Poverty was straightforward. There was no way to say 'I'm poor,' but to say 'I'm poor.'"**

Dancer, Rapper, and Actor

Tupac practiced his rhymes wherever he went. One day, while rhyming out loud in a San Francisco park, he saw Leila Steinberg, a teacher, reading an intriguing book. They talked and she became interested in the talented young man. Steinberg was no stranger to the hip-hop world; she was already managing other young rappers and had some important friends in the San Francisco hip-hop community. One of those friends was Atron Gregory, the manager of the Digital Underground, a local rap ensemble that included future stars Queen Latifah and Shock G. Steinberg arranged an **audition** for Tupac with Gregory, who was immediately impressed with the young rapper. He offered Tupac a job as a dancer and roadie. He would have to help carry equipment, load trucks, run errands, and do whatever other odd jobs he was assigned. Tupac jumped at the opportunity. Gregory also promised that, in time, Tupac would be given the chance to rap with the group.

That opportunity came in 1989 when Shock G invited Tupac to join him on stage to share the microphone. Soon after, Tupac provided vocals for the Digital Underground album *Sons of the P* and went on a world tour with the group. When the Digital Underground returned to California, Tupac had enough money to move out of the ghetto. With the money he'd earned on the tour, he rented an apartment and bought a car.

Tupac continued writing hard-edged gangsta rap and cut several **demo tapes**, hoping to get a record deal for a solo album. In the meantime, he learned that a movie producer was casting roles for the youth-oriented drama *Juice*. Tupac auditioned for a role and was immediately signed for the part. The producer, Neal Moritz, told *The Killing of Tupac Shakur* author Cathy Scott that Tupac was "dynamic, bold, powerful, magnetic—any word you want to use. Tupac was it. We cast him right on the spot."

Juice tells the story of three youths caught up in a double murder. Tupac played Bishop, one of the three lead roles. *New York Times* film critic Janet Maslin wrote that Tupac "becomes the film's most magnetic figure." He is so charismatic, in fact, that he undermines the message of the film. As the prime instigator of violence in the movie, Bishop should be the least sympathetic character, yet Tupac's portrayal draws the audience in. Said author Tony Patrick, director of a video biography of Tupac titled *Thug Immortal*:

> **There was something special about him. You saw it in his records. I saw it a little bit more in his movies. He had that glow. He had that charisma. There was no one else who looked like him. He had the eyebrows. He had the cheekbones. You know, handsome. Sometimes when you saw him sitting there introspective, if you were a woman you wanted to go over there and ask him, 'Pac, what's wrong? What can I do for you baby?' He had that special glow about him that attracted you to him right away.**

In 1992, Tupac appeared in *Juice*, a feature film about the lives of four young men growing up in Harlem. The low-budget movie was a financial success, earning more than $20 million, and many critics praised Tupac's performance.

In November 1991, Tupac's debut album, *2Pacalypse Now*, was released. Tupac's first single from the album, "Brenda's Got a Baby," focused on the issue of teen pregnancy. Other songs addressed such social problems as police brutality, poverty, and drug abuse.

When he returned to California after filming *Juice*, Tupac learned that Atron Gregory had swung a recording deal for him with Interscope Records, which agreed to release his first solo album. The record, *2pacalypse Now*, was released in 1991. It contained 13 songs about urban life. The songs depicted hostility between young blacks and police as well as violence against women. Most of the lyrics were laced with profanities. One song, "Brenda's Got a Baby," caused an uproar by referring to the murder of policemen. Vice President Dan Quayle condemned the song, saying it "has no place in our society."

The criticisms by Quayle and others helped generate **publicity** for the album, which encouraged many gangsta fans to see what this new rap star was all about. *2pacalypse Now* shot to the top of the hip-hop charts, eventually earning more than $90 million. Tupac Shakur had established himself as a true star on the rise in the hip-hop world. Director John Singleton said of him:

> **"Tupac spoke from a position that cannot be totally appreciated unless you understood the pathos of being a nigga, a displaced African soul, full of power, pain, and passion, with no focus or direction for all that energy except his art."**

Record producers vied for his talents, offering him lucrative contracts to record on their labels. But Tupac did not choose the path they offered. The path that he chose led him into the darkest and most violent corners of hip-hop culture.

Tupac Shakur spits at reporters after leaving a New York courthouse in July 1994. During the mid-1990s, despite his great success, the rapper had a series of run-ins with the law, and spent some time in prison.

3

Living the Gangsta Life

Tupac seemed determined to live up to the reputation of a law-breaking thug. Incidents involving fans, friends, and rivals led to a variety of charges. At one point, Tupac found himself scheduled to be in court in four cities—Los Angeles, Atlanta, New York, and Detroit—all within a period of two weeks.

Trouble seemed to follow him everywhere. Tupac had been cast for a role in the film *Menace II Society* but was fired because of violent outbursts on the set. Later, in 1993, Tupac met the film's directors on the set of a music video. Still harboring harsh feelings about being fired, he allegedly pulled a gun after a fight broke out. Tupac pled guilty to assault charges and was sentenced to 15 days in the Los Angeles County Jail and 15 days working for a road crew cleaning up California highways.

In 1994 Tupac served a brief jail sentence in East Lansing, Michigan, because of an incident the previous year during a concert at Michigan State

University. While on stage, a fight erupted between Tupac and another rapper. During the **melee**, he allegedly hit one of the performers with a baseball bat. Tupac eventually pled guilty and spent 10 days in the East Lansing lock-up.

According to Jeremy Miller, an editor at *The Source*, living out the life of a violent criminal was important for many rap artists. In order to sell albums, their audience had to believe that they rapped about their own lives. An artist from a middle-income suburban family rapping about the tough life in the ghetto would never have the same kind of credibility as a rapper convicted of violent crimes.

Success Despite the Turmoil

The mid-1990s may have been a lawless and violent time in Tupac Shakur's life, but it was also his most creative period. In 1993 Tupac's second album, *Strictly 4 My N.I.G.G.A.Z.*, was released by Interscope Records and quickly went **platinum**. The album covered many themes. There was a strong dose of the gangsta life—the title track spoke about murder and robbery—but there were also political and social messages. The single "Keep Ya Head Up" was a tribute to black women, who often found themselves the objects of abuse in gangsta rap songs. Tupac urged his listeners to respect women.

> **" I give a holler to my sisters on welfare**
> **Tupac cares, and don't nobody else care**
> **And uhh, I know they like to beat ya down a lot**
> **When you come around the block brothas clown a lot**
> **But please don't cry, dry your eyes, never let up**
> **Forgive but don't forget, girl keep your head up . . .**
> **I wonder why we take from our women**
> **While we rape our women**
> **Do we hate our women**
> **I think it's time we kill for our women**
> **Time we heal our women**
> **Be real to our women "**

On the track "Point The Finga" Tupac voiced his comments on police brutality and injustice, while his song "The Streetz R Death Row" spoke about the dismal fate faced by many young urban blacks as they grow up amid crime, drugs, and broken homes.

Tupac's second album, *Strictly 4 My N.I.G.G.A.Z.* (1993), was more successful than his debut, selling over a million copies. The album contained three hit singles: "Keep Ya Head Up," "Papa'z Song," and "I Get Around."

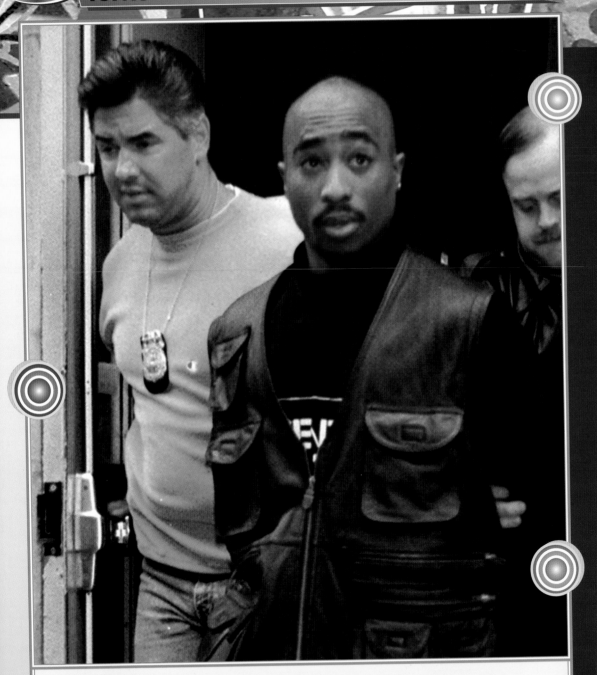

Police officers lead a handcuffed Tupac Shakur out of a Manhattan police station in November 1993. The rapper was arrested for a sexual attack on a woman. Although he denied the allegation, he was convicted of sexual assault the next year.

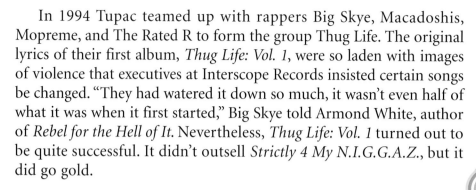

In 1994 Tupac teamed up with rappers Big Skye, Macadoshis, Mopreme, and The Rated R to form the group Thug Life. The original lyrics of their first album, *Thug Life: Vol. 1*, were so laden with images of violence that executives at Interscope Records insisted certain songs be changed. "They had watered it down so much, it wasn't even half of what it was when it first started," Big Skye told Armond White, author of *Rebel for the Hell of It*. Nevertheless, *Thug Life: Vol. 1* turned out to be quite successful. It didn't outsell *Strictly 4 My N.I.G.G.A.Z.*, but it did go gold.

Prison Days

In November 1993 Tupac and three other men were charged with raping a woman in a New York City hotel room. Tupac denied the accusation and claimed he was sleeping in an adjoining room when the assault took place. The case came to trial in November 1994, and Tupac was convicted of sexual assault, a lesser charge than rape. He was sentenced on February 14, 1995, to a lengthy prison term—one-and-a-half to four-and-a-half years. Tupac was taken to Clinton Correctional Facility, a maximum-security prison that houses New York State's most notorious and dangerous criminals.

While in prison, Tupac decided to improve his life. He read a great deal and told his visitors that he intended to give up the thug life when he was released. "I'm going to stop thugging," he told Jada Pinkett, according to author Michael Eric Dyson. "I am getting rid of the guns. . . . I'm changing, Jada. I don't want to do this rap thing anymore. I'm just going to act."

Few people came to visit Tupac in prison. However, Marion "Suge" Knight, a west coast rap producer, visited him quite often. Knight was the head of Death Row Records, a record label that specialized in the gangsta sound. Tupac was gangsta rap's biggest star, and Knight was anxious to add him to Death Row's pool of talent.

Despite earning millions from his first three albums and burgeoning acting career, Tupac had not saved any money. And his legal problems were costing him a great deal. His attorneys demanded large fees, and he was required to pay thousands of dollars in penalties to assault victims.

Knight offered Tupac a deal. He would assign Death Row's lawyers to his case and find a way to free him from jail, if, in return, Tupac would record his next three albums for Death Row. It was a commitment that would cost Knight more than a million dollars. According to author Cathy Scott, when Knight and Death Row attorney David Kenner sat down with Tupac and presented their terms, he answered, "I want to join the family. Just get me out."

A Dangerous Patron

Born in the ghetto of Compton, California, Suge Knight (the nickname was short for "Sugar Bear") played college football and briefly had a pro career. But he gave up football to work as a bodyguard for soul singer Bobby Brown. That experience introduced Knight to the music world, where he made important contacts.

In 1992 Knight had joined with the rapper and producer Dr. Dre to create their own independent record label, Death Row Records. Although Death Row was affiliated with a mainstream company, Interscope Records, Knight quickly surrounded himself with thugs and other tough characters from the streets. He reportedly used threats and intimidation to ensure that his label would succeed. "We called it Death Row 'cause most everybody had been involved with the law," he said. "A majority of our people was **parolees** or incarcerated. It's no joke."

Knight himself had many run-ins with the law, starting in 1987 when he allegedly shot a man outside his Las Vegas apartment and stole the victim's car. He pled guilty and was placed on **probation**. Three years later, he was charged with breaking a man's jaw and holding a gun to his face. Again, he was placed on probation. Additionally, Knight is said to have maintained close contact with a violent gang called the **Bloods**. He drove red cars, wore red suits, and even had the walls of his swimming pool painted red—an obvious show of allegiance to the gang, whose official color is red.

Knight was able to build Death Row into a thriving rap empire. He bought a fleet of luxury cars as well as sprawling estates in southern California and Las Vegas. He traveled to Vegas often, particularly when one of the large casino-hotels staged a heavyweight title fight. Knight frequently bought ringside tickets for himself and his friends, usually at prices that ran $1,000 or more a seat.

On October 12, 1995, attorneys working for Death Row Records won Tupac's freedom by posting $1.4 million bail while he waited for his appeal to come to trial. A Death Row limo stood waiting outside the prison to take him to a private jet, which then flew him across country to Los Angeles. That night, Tupac stepped into a Death Row studio to cut his first album for Suge Knight's record label.

Marion "Suge" Knight, head of Death Row Records, had a reputation as a dangerous and ruthless man. In 1995 he promised to help get Tupac out of prison if the rapper would make albums for Death Row.

On the Silver Screen

Although Tupac was in high demand among music producers, he also wanted to pursue an acting career. As his popularity as a rapper grew, film directors offered him roles in Hollywood productions. In 1993, Tupac starred as the romantic lead in a movie called *Poetic Justice*, which costarred the singer Janet Jackson. While generally considered a good movie, many critics felt *Poetic Justice* did not live up to the high standards set by director John Singleton's first movie, *Boyz N the Hood*. In contrast to the gangs and violence in his debut film, Singleton focused on personal relationships in *Poetic Justice*, using the crime, drugs, and poverty as a backdrop for his characters. Tupac's character Lucky, for example, manages to keep out of gangs only by working at a job that he despises. He dreams of more, but must simply endure.

Bullet (1996), a gangland story in which Tupac also played a drug dealer, got poor reviews. But it was followed up by the somewhat better

A publicity shot from the 1993 film *Poetic Justice*, which featured Tupac and Janet Jackson. The film, directed by John Singleton, was a box-office hit, and Tupac's strong performance was part of the reason. "Shakur makes a startlingly good impression," noted reviewer Tom Keogh.

movie *Gridlock'd* (1997), an offbeat movie, part-comedy, part-drama, in which Tupac was cast as a drug addict fighting to kick his habit. Film reviewer Roger Ebert called *Gridlock'd* Tupac's best performance.

Tupac's last film, *Gang Related* (1997), saw him play a corrupt detective alongside actor James Belushi. In it, Tupac played a cop who was involved in a drug scam. He and his partner would take drugs and a gun from the evidence room, sell the drugs to a dealer, then kill the dealer and take the money, both profiting and clearing the city of criminals. The last drug dealer they murdered, however, just so happened to be an undercover cop. The movie demanded complex and dark characters, and Tupac's performance was praised. As an actor, the young man displayed a natural talent that he would never fully get to explore.

Tupac (left) poses with Snoop Dogg (center) and Suge Knight (right) for a promotional photo. As one of Death Row's biggest stars, Tupac was drawn into a bitter feud between Knight and Sean "Puffy" Combs, the head of East Coast–based Bad Boy Entertainment.

4

East Coast vs. West Coast

upac Shakur's first album for Death Row was *All Eyez on Me*. It was a smash hit, selling more than 7 million copies. Many critics regard the double album as his best work. The album's theme set the stage for a year of violence that would become known as the East Coast–West Coast rap war.

Suge Knight did everything within his power to make *All Eyez on Me* a success—the album featured vocals by a number of other Death Row stars, including Snoop Dogg, Method Man, and Dr. Dre. Most of the album exalted crime, murder, and mayhem. There was even an attack on civil rights leader C. Delores Tucker, who had denounced gangsta rap because it preached the abuse of women and glorified violence.

On some of the album's tracks Tupac refers to himself as "Makaveli." This is a corruption of the name Niccolo Machiavelli, the 15th-century **philosopher** who argued that rulers must be willing to use cunning and deceit to gain and maintain power. In the track "When We Ride," Tupac suggests that he had also been inspired by such ruthless and unsavory rulers as Cuban dictator Fidel Castro, the Italian fascist Benito Mussolini, and Libyan president Muammar al-Qaddafi.

Puffy's Empire

As Suge Knight built Death Row into a powerful force in the rap world, another gangsta empire was growing on the east coast. In 1993 a young music producer named Sean "Puffy" Combs had founded the record label Bad Boy Entertainment. Based in New York, Bad Boy put out its own version of gangsta hip-hop. Bad Boy scored an enormous hit in 1994 with *Ready to Die*, the first album by six-foot-two-inch, 300-pound Biggie Smalls (who performed under the name Notorious B.I.G.). The album went platinum, but Suge Knight was unimpressed. He complained that Combs and Biggie had produced a poor imitation of Death Row's gangsta sound. For months, rappers from both organizations traded insults in the hip-hop press.

Tensions between the two record labels escalated in 1995 when Biggie and Combs attended *The Source* magazine's nationally televised Second Annual Hip-Hop Awards ceremony at a theater in New York. The Notorious B.I.G. had been named "Live Performer of the Year" by the magazine. Outside the theater, Biggie and Tupac encountered one another and exchanged angry words. Bodyguards for the two men were said to have exchanged blows, and someone reportedly brandished a gun.

A few weeks later, Biggie and Combs attended the same party in Atlanta, Georgia, as Knight and his friend and employee Jake Robles. During the party an altercation erupted, and Robles was shot and killed. Knight blamed Combs for arranging the murder—an accusation that Combs denied. No one was ever arrested in the case.

To fan the flames of the rivalry, in early 1996 Tupac released a single titled "Hit 'Em Up." The lyrics insulted Biggie and also suggested that Tupac had seduced Biggie's wife, the singer Faith Evans. That March at the Soul Train Music Awards in Los Angeles, Tupac's album *Me Against the World* was named "Best Rap Album." When he went onstage to collect the award, Tupac insulted Combs and Bad Boy Entertainment. Biggie, who had performed during the awards show, encountered Tupac backstage and caused a row. Newspapers reported that Tupac threatened Biggie with a gun, but both men denied the charge.

Notorious B.I.G. emerged as star on the hip-hop scene with the release of his first album, *Ready to Die*, in 1994. The rivalry between Biggie and Tupac grew more bitter throughout 1995, as each rapper insulted the other in his lyrics.

Combs tried to downplay the rivalry, claiming to reporters that there was no East Coast–West Coast rap war. He told *USA Today*:

"I think people have a misconception that first of all we were in a feud. I don't think you can be in a feud with somebody if there's not two people arguing. I mean, I've never had a problem with Tupac or a problem with Suge Knight or a problem with Death Row, a problem with anybody in the industry, for that matter. The only thing I've heard is the records that you've heard. I've never been approached on any other level besides that. So it was more hype than anything."

According to Russell Simmons, CEO of the rap label Def Jam Records, there wasn't an East Coast–West Coast rivalry so much as a Death Row–Bad Boy rivalry that was spun by the media into a much larger problem. "The war was created and fueled by our own radio stations and our own [hip-hop] magazines," Simmons told *Spin* magazine.

A Quick and Brutal End

On the night of September 7, 1996, Suge Knight and Tupac Shakur attended a heavyweight match between boxers Mike Tyson and Bruce Seldon at the MGM Grand Hotel in Las Vegas. Knight and Tupac left the arena with plans to attend a party at a Las Vegas nightspot known as Club 662. The party had been organized by the Las Vegas Police Department as a fundraiser for Barry's Boxing Gym, an organization that hoped to give kids an alternative to violence on the street. Suge Knight had helped with the event so that Tupac could participate as part of his court-ordered community service.

As Tupac, Knight, and their two bodyguards from the Bloods walked through the lobby of the MGM Grand, one of the bodyguards spotted a man named Orlando Anderson, who was a member of a rival gang, the **Crips**. Tupac and the two Bloods attacked Anderson, knocking him to the floor. Knight also waded into the scuffle, although he claimed later to have been trying to break up the fight.

After beating up Anderson, Tupac, Knight, and the bodyguards left the hotel lobby. Suge and Tupac headed to Club 662 in a BMW sedan. The bodyguards entered a separate car and followed. It was a hot night, so the windows of the BMW were rolled down, and hip-hop

Bad Boy Entertainment CEO Sean Combs (left) is pictured with former Def Jam Records executive Russell Simmons in a 2002 photo. Combs attempted to downplay the East Coast–West Coast rivalry, but was unable to prevent the war of words from turning violent.

blasted on the car stereo. While Knight waited for a light to turn green at the intersection of Flamingo Road and Koval Lane, a late-model Cadillac carrying three or four men pulled alongside his BMW. Suddenly, one of the men in the backseat of the Cadillac stuck a gun out of the left window and fired 13 shots.

Tupac tried to seek protection in the backseat, but he had his seatbelt on and was unable to move. Suge threw himself over Tupac to try

the killing of Tupac Shakur

The cover of the book *The Killing of Tupac Shakur* shows the rapper in a car with Suge Knight just before the shooting. Tupac Shakur died in a hospital on September 13, 1996, six days after being gunned down on the streets of Las Vegas.

to protect him and was slashed by broken glass. Tupac was hit three times: bullets pierced his chest, hip, and right hand. Miraculously, Knight did not sustain any bullet wounds. His most serious wound was from a fragment of glass from the windshield that hit him in the back of the neck.

Knight asked Tupac, "You hit?"

"I'm hit," Tupac answered.

As the Cadillac drove away, Knight hit the BMW's accelerator, wrestled the car into a U-turn, and told Tupac, "You need a hospital, Pac. I'm gonna get you to a hospital right now."

Knight didn't get far. Two shots had been fired into the BMW's tires, and the Las Vegas streets were snarled with traffic. He sped the car through red lights and over medians until it got stuck on a curb. Two bicycle police had heard the shots and radioed for backup and an ambulance. Rather than follow the shooters, they followed Suge's BMW; the authorities had no idea what had happened beyond the sounds of gunfire. Unfortunately, their decision meant that the crime scene was not secured. Pedestrians were allowed to contaminate the scene for about 20 minutes before officers arrived, and potential witnesses were lost as they left to carry on their night. When the police caught up with Knight, they treated him like a suspect until a bodyguard explained what had happened.

Knight's car was covered in blood, and Tupac's shirt had become completely soaked. Suge and a bodyguard lifted him from the car as the paramedics arrived. Tupac was rushed to a nearby hospital, where he fell into a **coma**. Tupac lingered for six days and then died. He was twenty-five years old.

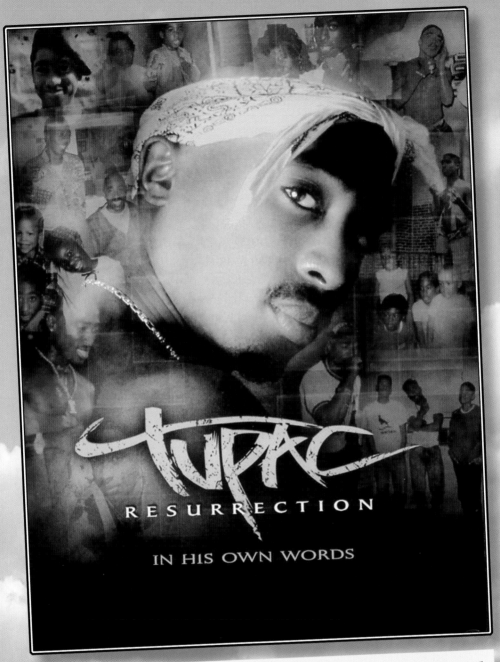

In 2003, the documentary *Tupac: Resurrection* was released. The film is narrated by Tupac, using excerpts from old interviews, and includes many rare or unpublished photos and video clips. It was nominated for an Academy Award.

Improving the Lives of Others

The East Coast–West Coast rivalry did not end with the murder of Tupac. Biggie Smalls was immediately suspected of having been involved because of their feud. Six months after Tupac was gunned down, the Notorious B.I.G. was killed while sitting in a car on a Los Angeles street. Some people believed the murder was reprisal for Tupac's death.

In the early morning hours of March 9, 1997, Biggie Smalls had just left a party when a black Chevrolet Impala pulled alongside his car and opened fire. Biggie had been listening to a tape of his new album, *Life After Death*, which was scheduled for release in two weeks.

Since their deaths both Biggie Smalls and Tupac Shakur have continued to earn millions of dollars for their record labels. During the 11 months that Tupac recorded for Death Row before his death, he produced dozens of songs. It is believed that on occasion, he recorded as many as three songs in a single day. Just a few weeks after the fatal shooting, Death Row released an album under Tupac's favorite alias, Makaveli, titled *Makaveli: The Don Killuminati: The 7 Day Theory*.

Since its release, the album has sparked rumors about Tupac's death. Some rumors have suggested that the rap star faked his death

A family shops for Tupac's music in an Ohio record store shortly after the rapper's death in September 1996. Tupac is the best-selling hip-hop artist of all time, with more than 40 million albums sold worldwide.

Pedestrians walk past a wall mural featuring Tupac Shakur on the lower east side of Manhattan. Many conspiracy theories about Tupac's death have circulated over the years; to this day, questions remain about the identity of his murderer.

and is living under an assumed name. Rearranging the letters of *Makaveli: The Don Killuminati: The 7 Day Theory*, theorists come up with the sentence, "OK on the 7th u think I'm dead, yet I'm really alive." Other people believe the album contains a clue to Tupac's murder. On the first track, "Intro/Bomb First (My Second Reply)," some listeners reported hearing the words, "Suge shot me."

After Tupac's death, Afeni Shakur won control of most of her son's unreleased music, and formed a music label to oversee the production of posthumous albums. Since 1996, numerous albums of his music have been officially released.

Adding to the conspiracy theory is a music video that Tupac filmed for the single "I Ain't Mad at Cha," which wasn't released until 1998 when it was added to the *2Pac's Greatest Hits* album. The video includes a scene in which Shakur is shot and killed, followed by a scene depicting his ascent to heaven.

After the release of *Makaveli: The Don Killuminati: The 7 Day Theory*, Afeni Shakur won a court order awarding her the rights to 150 of her son's songs. Following Tupac's death, Afeni Shakur started Amaru Records to produce her son's records. She insists on total control of his music.

Murders Never Solved

The murders of Tupac Shakur and Biggie Smalls have never been solved. In 2002, the *Los Angeles Times* published a series of stories suggesting that Biggie paid Orlando Anderson, the Crip who Tupac attacked in the lobby of the MGM Grand, $1 million to commit the murder. The stories indicated that Biggie even gave Anderson a gun with which to commit the murder. Before his own death, Biggie had vehemently denied any involvement in Tupac's murder. After the newspaper series was published, members of Biggie's family issued a statement that read, "This false story is a disrespect to not only our family but the family of Tupac Shakur. Both men will have no peace as long as stories such as these continue to be written."

Rolling Stone journalist Randall Sullivan has published stories with a different theory. His articles in 2001 and 2005 alleged that Knight ordered both murders, which were then carried out by Los Angeles police officers on the Death Row payroll. Sullivan quoted sources contending that Tupac was murdered because Knight owed him $3 million and did not want to pay. The story reported that Smalls was killed because Knight wanted to rob Puffy Combs of his biggest star.

Knight has denied the accusations. Shortly after Tupac's death, Knight told *Time* magazine that despite its celebration of violence, gangsta rap continues to tell the true story of lives led by many young blacks in urban America. "I don't want to give up gangsta rap, not at all," he said. "It's not about us. It's about the community; it's about our people, and we can't turn our backs on them."

Softening His Image

A decade after the deaths of Tupac and Biggie, their cases continue to make headlines. Voletta Wallace, the mother of the Notorious B.I.G., filed a lawsuit against the Los Angeles Police Department alleging that, as Sullivan reported, rogue police officers had participated in the murder of her son. The case came to trial in 2005, but was delayed after a judge ruled that the Los Angeles police had withheld valuable evidence from Voletta Wallace's attorneys, and ordered the city to pay $1.1 million.

Unlike Biggie's mother, Afeni Shakur has not searched for her son's killer. "Not even a nanosecond have I concerned myself with who shot him or why they shot him, or what should happen to them," Afeni Shakur told the Associated Press. "I spend my time putting my son's work out, because, guess what—they shot him [but] did not shut him up."

Afeni Shakur has total creative control over the production of her son's albums. And she has used her power to soften his image as a hard-core gangsta. In late 2004, Amaru Records released the ninth album since Tupac Shakur's death, *Loyal to the Game*. The cover of the album depicts Tupac, dressed in white, wearing glasses and sitting quietly with his head cocked to the side, deep in thought.

The rap star Eminem was recruited to help produce the album. Eminem set the rhymes to beats he often uses on his own records and invited some contemporary rappers to add vocals. He convinced pop star Elton John to sing on the album as well. A large portion of *Loyal to the Game* depicts gangsta life in the way that made Tupac a star, but some of the tracks look beyond thugging. "Ghetto Gospel" includes a message of hope about overcoming life's obstacles.

In the decade since his death, Tupac has remained an enormously popular recording star. His albums have sold more than 40 million copies, most of which were sold following his death. When *Loyal to the Game* was released, it debuted at the top of the hip-hop charts.

Afeni's Responsibility

In life, Tupac Shakur was a brilliant artist, but his acceptance of the gangsta life led to numerous scrapes with the law, imprisonment, and, ultimately, his own death. Afeni Shakur believes that in death her son can set a better example for young people. Using the money she has earned from the sale of his records, Afeni established the Tupac Amaru Shakur Foundation in Stone Mountain, Georgia. The foundation supports the Tupac Amaru Shakur Center for the Arts, which provides education in the performing arts for students between the ages of

XXI

WE DONE DONE IT AGAIN

Tupac Amaru Shakur
1971-1996 R.I.P.

2PAC
THUG HOLIDAY

**Another Tribute to Hip-Hop's
Most Influential MC**

SUGE KNIGHT Remembers his soldier
SHOCK-G The man who put him on
ATLANTA SHOOTOUT Two cops got bucked

PLUS: KHIA ★ ANGIE MARTINEZ ★ CLIPSE
BERNIE MAC ★ THE NEW XZIBIT LP

Tupac Shakur remains incredibly popular, and articles about him or tributes to his music continue to appear in hip-hop publications. In polls done by MTV (2003) and *Vibe* magazine (2004), hip-hop fans rated Tupac the greatest MC of all time.

A bronze statue of the rapper stands in the Peace Garden at the Tupac Amaru Shakur Center for the Arts in Atlanta. "Every generation picks their own heroes," sculptor Tina Allen said at the unveiling ceremony. "This generation's hero is clearly Tupac Shakur."

12 and 18. Students who attend the center's day camp take classes in creative writing, voice, acting, stage and set design, and poetry. The foundation sponsors nationwide essay competitions and awards scholarships to help students attend colleges.

Visitors to the center can tour galleries that feature artwork inspired by Tupac's music as well as the awards won by the rapper. A seven-foot-tall bronze statue of Tupac has been erected in the Peace Garden that surrounds the center in the hilly Georgia countryside.

In an interview with the Associated Press, Afeni Shakur said that if her son had lived, it is likely he would have left the gangsta life and used his talents to improve the lives of others. Now that he is dead, she said, it is her duty to carry out that responsibility. "We have a list of things that Tupac left for us to do, so all we're doing is going over that list, going down that list, checking them off. So, at the end of the day, we'll be able to say we've done fulfilled our responsibility to an incredible human being."

1971   Lesane Parish Crooks is born on June 16 in New York City; his mother, Afeni Shakur, soon changes his name to Tupac Amaru Shakur.

1983   Twelve-year-old Tupac appears in the play *A Raisin in the Sun* at the Apollo Theater in Harlem, New York.

1985   Afeni Shakur moves her family to Baltimore, where Tupac enrolls as a student at the Baltimore School for the Arts.

1988   Fearing violence in the family's Baltimore neighborhood, Afeni Shakur sends her son across country to live with friends in Marin City, California.

1989   While rapping in a San Francisco park, Tupac meets Leila Steinberg, who is impressed with his talent and introduces him to rap promoter Atron Gregory.

1990   Tupac joins the rap group Digital Underground as a dancer and roadie, but is soon given the chance to rap with the group.

1991   Tupac's first solo album, *2Pacalypse Now*, is released and soars to the top of the hip-hop charts.

1992   Tupac makes his screen acting debut by playing a leading role in the film *Juice*.

1993   Tupac's second album, *Strictly 4 My N.I.G.G.A.Z.* released; meanwhile, his trouble with the law begins when he is charged in Michigan for assaulting another rapper with a baseball bat. Tupac is also accused of sexual assault by a New York woman.

1994   In November, Tupac is shot five times while entering the lobby of a recording studio in New York; he survives the shooting and leaves the hospital early so that he may hear the verdict in the sex assault case. He is convicted.

1995   In February, Tupac begins serving his sentence in prison on the sexual assault conviction. He is granted early parole in October through the intercession of Death Row Records founder Marion "Suge" Knight, who signs him to a recording contract.

1996   His first Death Row album, *All Eyez on Me*, is released and goes platinum. On September 7, Tupac and Suge Knight are ambushed in their car on a Las Vegas street. Tupac dies a week later.

1997   Afeni Shakur founds the Tupac Amaru Shakur Foundation to provide education in the arts for young people; Suge Knight begins a five-year jail term for his role in the assault on Orlando Anderson, a member of the Crips street gang; Biggie Smalls is murdered on a Los Angeles street.

2001   *Rolling Stone* publishes a story suggesting that Suge Knight had Tupac murdered to avoid paying the rapper a $3 million debt.

2002   *The Los Angeles Times* publishes a series of stories alleging that Biggie Smalls paid $1 million to Orlando Anderson to kill Tupac.

2003   The doumentary *Tupac: Resurrection*, narrated in Tupac's voice, is released.

2004   *Loyal to the Game* released by Amaru Records, the record label started by Afeni Shakur to produce her son's music.

2005   *The Rose, Volume 2*, an album featuring Tupac's poetry set to music, is released.

2005   *Tupac: Resurrection* is nominated for an Academy Award as Best Documentary.

Discography
Albums
1991   *2Pacalypse Now*
1993   *Strictly 4 My N.I.G.G.A.Z.*
1994   *Thug Life: Thug Life Vol. 1*
1995   *Me Against the World*
1996   *All Eyez on Me*

Released Posthumously
1996   *Makaveli: The Don Killuminati: 7 Day Theory*
1997   *R U Still Down*
1998   *2Pac's Greatest Hits*
1999   *Still I Rise*
2000   *The Rose that Grew from Concrete*
2001   *Until the End of Time*
2002   *Better Dayz*
2003   *Tupac: Resurrection*
2004   *Loyal to the Game*
2005   *The Rose, Volume 2*

Films
1992   *Juice*
1993   *Poetic Justice*
1994   *Above the Rim*
1996   *Bullet*
1997   *Gridlock'd*
        Gang Related
2002   *Biggie and Tupac*, documentary
2003   *Tupac: Resurrection*, documentary

Books of Poetry
1999   *The Rose that Grew from Concrete*
2004   *Inside a Thug's Heart*

Awards and Recognition
1994   Nominated for an American Music Award as
        Favorite Rap/Hip-Hop Artist.

1996   Nominated for Grammy Awards for Best Rap Album
        for *Me Against the World* and Best Rap Solo
        Performance for "Dear Mama."

Nominated for an MTV Video Music Award for Best Rap Video for "California Love."

Winner of Soul Train Music Award for Best Rap Album for *Me Against the World.*

1997 Winner of an American Music Award as Favorite Rap/Hip-Hop Artist for *Makaveli: The Don Killuminati: 7 Day Theory.*

Nominated for Grammy Awards for Best Rap Album for *All Eyez on Me*, and Best Rap Performance for "California Love" and "How Do U Want It."

1999 Nominated for an MTV Video Music Award for Best Rap Video for "Changes."

2000 Nominated for a Grammy Award for Best Rap Solo Performance for "Changes."

2002 Inducted into the Hip-Hop Hall of Fame.

2003 Selected by *Access Hollywood* as one of the 10 most important musicians in history; the list also includes such stars as Elvis Presley, Bob Dylan, Frank Sinatra, and Madonna.

Selected by MTV as one of 50 Greatest Rappers.

2005 *Tupac Resurrection*, which was narrated in Tupac's voice, nominated for an Academy Award as Best Documentary.

Books

Alexander, Frank, and Heidi Siegmund Cuda. *Got Your Back: Protecting Tupac in the World of Gangsta Rap.* New York: St. Martin's Griffin, 2000.

Ardis, Angela, and Tupac Shakur. *Inside a Thug's Heart.* New York: Dafina, 2004.

Dyson, Michael Eric. *Holler if You Hear Me: Searching for Tupac Shakur.* New York: Basic Civitas Books, 2001.

Scott, Cathy. *The Killing of Tupac Shakur.* Las Vegas: Huntington Press, 2002.

———. *The Murder of Biggie Smalls.* New York: St. Martin's Press, 2000.

Shakur, Tupac. *The Rose That Grew From Concrete.* New York: MTV/Pocket Books, 1999.

White, Armond. *Rebel for the Hell of It: The Life of Tupac Shakur.* New York: Thunder Mouth's Press, 1997.

Periodicals

Farley, Christopher John. "From the Driver's Side: Gangsta-Rap Mogul 'Suge' Knight Finally Breaks His Silence on Tupac Shakur's Unsolved Murder." *Time* 148, no. 16 (Sept. 30, 1996): p. 70.

Moody, Nekesha Mumbi. "A Mother's Mission: Afeni Shakur Keeps Slain Tupac's Legacy Vibrant." *Albany Times Union,* Nov. 13, 2003.

Sullivan, Randall. *LAbyrinth: A Detective Investigates the Murders of Tupac Shakur and Notorious B.I.G.* New York: Atlantic Monthly Press, 2002.

Web Sites

http://www.tasf.org
Internet site of the Tupac Amaru Shakur Foundation.

http://www.deathrowrecords.net
Formerly known as Death Row Records, Tha Row released Tupac Shakur's final record before his death.

http://foia.fbi.gov/foiaindex/cripsbloods.htm
An extensive archive of newspaper and magazine stories on the Crips and Bloods, maintained by the Federal Bureau of Investigation.

http://www.2paclegacy.com
Official website maintained by Afeni Shakur, Tupac Shakur's mother.

audition—opportunity for actor to win a role in a play or movie, or for a musician or singer to be selected to perform.

Bloods—a nationwide gang originally from Los Angeles. Gang members usually identify themselves with red bandanas, although cliques within the gang may use different colors.

coma—a prolonged state of deep inconsciousness.

Crips—a nationwide gang originally from Los Angeles. Gang members usually identify themselves with blue bandanas.

demo tape—a recording made to give music producers and others an idea of how a new song might sound. These are often made on simple recording equipment with minimal instrumentation.

destitute—state of extreme poverty.

ghetto—depressed area of an inner city where poor people are forced to live because they lack the means to improve their lives.

introspection—a detailed mental self-examination of feelings, thoughts, and motives.

lyrics—words of a song.

MC—short for "master of ceremonies," in hip-hop culture this term is used to describe someone who raps using rhymed verses to compliment the work of a DJ (disc jockey).

melee—large and confusing fight in which many people participate.

parolee—a prisoner who is granted parole, or permitted to leave jail before his or her entire sentence has been served.

philosopher—intellectual, often a writer, who seeks wisdom and offers theories on ethics and other issues that affect people's lives.

platinum—a record industry designation for an album that has sold more than a million copies.

probation—status granted to a criminal defendant that permits him or her to serve a sentence outside jail.

prosecution—attorneys working for the government who present the case against a criminal defendant during a trial.

publicity—information published in newspapers and magazines or aired on radio and television calling attention to a person or issue.

Hal Marcovitz is a journalist who has written more than 70 books for young readers as well as the satirical novel *Painting the White House*. He lives in Chalfont, Pennsylvania, with his wife, Gail, and daughters Ashley and Michelle.

Picture Credits

page

 2: Zuma Press/Michel Haddi/eyevine
 8: Zuma Press/Michel Haddi/eyevine
11: UPI/Jim Ruymen
13: Zuma Press/Jane Caine
14: KRT/David Handschuh
16: Paramount/Everrett Collection
19: WENN
21: WENN
22: Paramount/Everrett Collection
25: Paramount/Everrett Collection
26: UPI/Chi Modu
28: AP Photo/Bebeto Matthews
31: WENN
32: AP Photo/Justin Sutcliffe

35: KRT/Chuck Fadely
36: Columbia Pictures/
    Everrett Collection
38: NMI/Death Row Records
41: KRT/Death Row Records
43: Zuma Press/NYPP
44: NMI/Mechell Feng
46: NMI/Paramount Pictures
48: KRT/Jocelyn Williams
49: UPI/Ezio Petersen
50: Zuma Press/Rena Durham
53: NMI/Mechell Feng
54: PRNews Foto/NMI

Front cover: Zuma Press/Toronto Star
Back cover: AFP/Death Row Records